Lincoln Branch Library
1221 E. 7 Mile
Detroit, MI 48203

D0929350

OCT -- 2002
L I

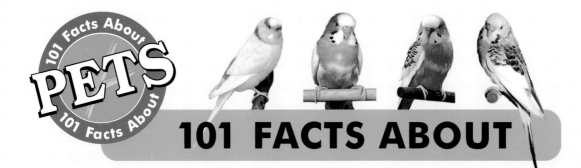

101 Facts About Pets
101 Facts About

101 FACTS ABOUT

PARAKEETS

Please visit our web site at: www.garethstevens.com
For a free color catalog describing Gareth Stevens Publishing's
list of high-quality books and multimedia programs,
call 1-800-542-2595 or fax your request to (414) 332-3567.

Library of Congress Cataloging-in-Publication Data

Barnes, Julia.
   101 facts about parakeets / by Julia Barnes. — North American ed.
       p. cm. — (101 facts about pets)
   Includes bibliographical references and index.
   Summary: Describes the history, physical characteristics, and behavior of parakeets,
and presents information on choosing, training, and caring for one as a pet.
     ISBN 0-8368-3020-2 (lib. bdg.)
     1. Budgerigar—Miscellanea—Juvenile literature. [1. Parakeets. 2. Pets.]
   I. Title: One hundred one facts about parakeets. II. Title. III. Series.
   SF473.B8B26   2002
   636.6'864—dc21   2001049678

This North American edition first published in 2002 by
Gareth Stevens Publishing
A World Almanac Education Group Company
330 West Olive Street, Suite 100
Milwaukee, WI 53212 USA

This U.S. edition © 2002 by Gareth Stevens, Inc. Original edition © 2001 by Ringpress Books
Limited. First published by Ringpress Books Limited, P.O. Box 8, Lydney, Gloucestershire,
GL15 4YN, United Kingdom. Additional end matter © 2002 by Gareth Stevens, Inc.

Ringpress Series Editor: Claire Horton-Bussey
Ringpress Designer: Sara Howell
Gareth Stevens Editors: Jim Mezzanotte and Mary Dykstra

All rights reserved to Gareth Stevens, Inc. No part of this book may be reproduced, stored
in a retrieval system, or transmitted in any form or by any means, electronic, mechanical,
photocopying, recording, or otherwise, without the prior written permission of the publisher,
except for the inclusion of brief quotations in an acknowledged review.

Printed in Hong Kong through Printworks Int. Ltd

1 2 3 4 5 6 7 8 9 06 05 04 03 02

101 FACTS ABOUT

PARAKEETS

Julia Barnes

Gareth Stevens Publishing
A WORLD ALMANAC EDUCATION GROUP COMPANY

1 The beautiful parakeet, with its colorful feathers and interesting personality, is popular as a pet bird around the world. Parakeets are part of the parrot family.

2 The most common pet parakeet is called the budgerigar, or "budgie," for short. Budgies are native to Australia, where they live in dry grasslands.

3 In the wild, large flocks of budgies fly together, searching for food. In 1770, when Captain James Cook was exploring Australia, he reported seeing flocks of budgies so large that the birds covered the Sun as they flew overhead.

4 When early settlers in Australia asked the native Aborigines what they called these little green birds, the Aborigines replied "betchery-gah," which became the word "budgerigar."

budgie is only 4 inches (10 centimeters) long from its head to the tip of its tail. A pet budgie can be twice that size, or even bigger.

7 All wild budgies have light green feathers, so they can blend in with plants and trees around them.

5 Years later, when experts translated the Aboriginal word, they discovered that "betchery-gah" means "good to eat!"

6 Wild budgies are much smaller than the tame budgies sold as pets. A wild

8 In the wild, budgies will make their nests in the branches or trunks of trees. They hollow out a space where a female budgie, or hen, can lay her eggs.

9 In 1840, the budgie was first brought to Europe. A budgie with all-yellow feathers was first hatched there in the year 1872.

10 Soon **breeders** were raising and selling budgies of many different colors. There are now more than 60 different colors of budgies, as well as hundreds of patterns and color combinations.

11 The basic colors of parakeets are blue, white, green, and yellow.

12 Each basic color, however, can have many different shades. For example, a parakeet might be sky blue, cobalt blue, or mauve.

6

13 A **lutino** parakeet is yellow with white wing tips and tail feathers. An **albino** parakeet has no color. It is completely white, with pink eyes and feet.

14 **Pied** parakeets have patches or bands of either yellow and green or blue and white. No two pied parakeets ever look exactly the same.

15 A **crested** parakeet (left) is a variety of parakeet that has a fringe of feathers going around its head, while **tufted** varieties of parakeets have crests of feathers sticking up at the front of the head.

16 Breeders are still developing new varieties of parakeets with different colors and patterns. For example, a **spangled** parakeet (right) has a solid color on the body and pale wings with dark edges.

17 No matter what kind of colors or patterns parakeets have, they are easy to care for and fun to watch.

18 Like all birds, the parakeet is **warm-blooded**. It breathes quickly to cool down and fluffs up its feathers to stay warm.

19 A parakeet's body is covered with small contour feathers, and its wings are covered with flight feathers that help it fly. The parakeet uses its long tail feathers to steer while flying.

20 At least once a year, parakeets will **molt**, or shed, their feathers. New feathers grow in to replace the ones that are lost.

21 The parakeet has very good eyesight. A parakeet's eyes are located on either side of its head, so the bird can see to the side as well as to the front.

22 Parakeets have three eyelids. Besides the upper and lower eyelids, they have lids that can be pulled across the eyes for protection.

23 When a parakeet goes to sleep, the bird stands on one leg with its eyes closed and its head tucked under one of its wings.

24 A parakeet uses its curved beak to crack open seeds, to climb, and to **preen**, or clean its feathers.

25 A parakeet can imitate human speech. The male birds, or cocks, are better "talkers" than the females.

26 A parakeet named "Puck," which lived in California, knew a record-breaking 1,782 words before his death in 1994.

27 Another famous parakeet, "Sparkie Williams," could recite eight nursery rhymes and say 500 different words.

28 The average life span of a parakeet is seven or eight years, but some parakeets have been known to live much longer.

29 The longest-living budgie on record is "Charlie," who lived in England until the ripe old age of 29!

30 You should buy a parakeet that is between seven and eight weeks of age, so it is easy to tame.

or a hen. At three to four months in age, the cere changes from pale purple to blue in cocks and to brown in hens.

31 Until the age of three months, a parakeet has a wavy black pattern on its head called **barring** (above). This pattern reaches down to its **cere**, the fleshy area above its beak.

32 It is not easy to tell whether a young budgie is a cock

33 You will need expert advice when you choose your parakeet, so make sure you go to a pet store that specializes in bird care.

35 When selecting a parakeet, you should look for the following signs of good health.

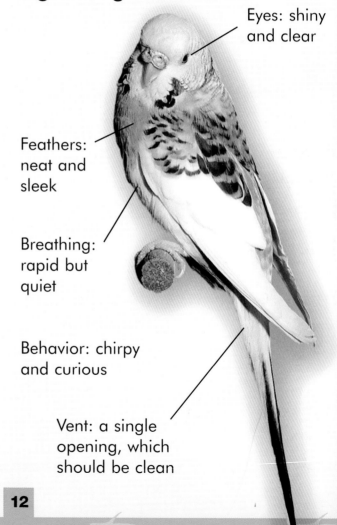

Eyes: shiny and clear

Feathers: neat and sleek

Breathing: rapid but quiet

Behavior: chirpy and curious

Vent: a single opening, which should be clean

34 If you want to buy an unusual type of parakeet, you will probably have to go to a breeder.

36 Your parakeet will need a good home, so set up its cage before you choose your pet.

37 You can keep your pet parakeets in a regular bird cage, in a large indoor enclosure called a **flight**, or in an outside **aviary** (below) that can house many birds.

38 Some experts feel that you should buy two parakeets so they will not get lonely. Try to choose two males or two females.

39 When you are choosing a cage, purchase the biggest that will fit in your home (above).

40 Parakeets fly from side to side, not up and down. Experts say you should use a cage at least 20 inches (50 cm) long.

41 Parakeets are good climbers. Your pet will get plenty of exercise climbing on the horizontal bars of its cage.

42 Place your parakeet's cage out of direct sunlight, in a location away from cold drafts of air, which could make your pet sick.

43 If you plan to keep a large number of parakeets, a garden aviary provides a wonderful, natural home.

46 Small branches of different sizes can be used as perches. The best perches for a parakeet are at least 3/8 inch (10 mm) wide.

44 An aviary provides parakeets with a weatherproof shelter where they can go at night or in bad weather.

47 You can cut branches from many kinds of trees for perches. Do not use branches from trees that have recently been sprayed.

45 You will need to outfit your bird's cage with several perches, each set at a different height.

48 Cover the bottom of the cage with paper and wood shavings or with sand sheets, which are available in most pet stores.

51 Parakeets are active birds. They like to move from perch to perch and use ladders and swings.

52 You can buy a variety of parakeet toys, such as rings and balls, in a pet store or supermarket. Parakeets also enjoy playing with small wooden balls and empty thread spools.

49 Put an automatic feeder, sometimes called a seed hopper, on the side of the cage. Be sure the feeder is not under a perch, where it would get dirty.

50 Give your bird a fresh supply of water daily in a bottle attached to the side of the cage.

16

Parakeets cannot preen, or clean, their feathers (below) very well if their feathers are not wet.

53 Put a different toy in the cage each day to give your pet plenty of variety.

56 A number of seed mixes are sold just for parakeets. They contain the vitamins and minerals that parakeets need.

54 Your bird will like to splash around in a birdbath hooked to the side of the cage or in a dish of water.

55 Bathing and splashing around in water serves a very useful purpose.

57 Most parakeet seed mixes contain millet seeds, which are round, and canary seeds, which are somewhat oval. Some mixes also contain linseed, or niger.

58 Parakeets break open seeds with their beaks. The bird eats the inner part of each seed, called the **kernel**. The outer part, the **husk**, is left behind.

59 You need to remove the leftover husks every day before giving your parakeet more seed. Some parakeet owners clear out the husks by blowing on the food container.

60 In addition to seeds, parakeets need fresh fruit and vegetables. Favorites include apples, carrots, lettuce and spinach. Wash the fresh foods, chop them into large chunks, and place a handful on the floor of the cage.

61 Some parakeets like to chew on a piece of apple or carrot stuck between the bars of the cage.

62 Your bird will enjoy pecking seeds off a spray, or stalk, of millet (right). Millet is an energy food for birds.

63 Since parakeets do not have teeth, they swallow grit (below) to help them digest the tough seeds they eat.

64 The grit mixes in with the seeds, which parakeets swallow whole. The grit helps grind up the food in the **gizzard**, which is near the stomach.

65 Parakeets should also have minerals in their diet to stay healthy. Attach a small piece of cuttlefish bone (above) to the side of your parakeet's cage to provide calcium, and place a small mineral block (right) in the cage to provide your pet with iodine.

19

cage. You should also check your bird's water bottle daily.

68 Clean the cage and its contents about once a week. Wipe the bars of the cage with a cloth and warm, soapy water. Be sure that the bowl of grit is full.

66 Apart from feeding your parakeet, your most important job is to keep its home clean.

67 Change the paper or sand sheets on the bottom of the cage every day. Clear out seed husks and throw away any other food that has been left in the

69 Parakeets are hardy little birds, and with a good diet and clean housing, they will experience few health problems.

70 Still, it is a good idea to find a veterinarian in your area who specializes in treating birds.

74 If your parakeet's beak gets too long, your pet will not be able to pick up seeds, so this condition needs immediate attention. Your veterinarian can clip the beak for you.

71 Check your bird's claws from time to time. Your pet's claws should wear down naturally if you provide a variety of perches.

72 If your parakeet's claws get too long, ask your veterinarian to trim them for you.

73 Gnawing on bark and the cuttlefish bone usually keeps your bird's beak from growing too long.

21

75 If you already have a parakeet and then get another one, be sure to keep them in separate cages for several weeks.

76 You want to be sure the new parakeet is healthy before it comes in contact with your other bird. The new bird also needs time to adjust to its surroundings.

77 At first, let your parakeets see and hear each other from a distance. Then move the two birds into the same cage.

78 When you get a new parakeet, give it several days to settle into its new surroundings before you attempt to handle it.

its perch so the bird will be able to hop onto your hand.

79 After a few days, you can start training your bird to sit on your finger. Start by carefully opening the cage door with one hand, using the other hand to block the opening so your bird cannot escape.

80 Holding a piece of millet spray in your hand, slowly put your hand into the parakeet's cage near

81 Hold your hand very still and wait for your parakeet to hop onto your hand to get at the seeds.

82 Eventually, your parakeet will learn to use your finger as a handheld perch.

83 Do not rush making friends with your bird. You may find it helpful to talk to your parakeet and gently stroke its feathers, so it learns to trust you.

86 Before taking your bird out of its cage, be sure the house is safe. First, close the doors and windows so your pet cannot escape.

84 After your parakeet has gotten used to perching on your finger inside the cage, you can take your pet out of its cage.

85 If your pet starts to raise its wings, stop moving until it settles down. If you point your finger slightly upward, your bird will move to the highest point of its traveling perch.

87 Close the curtains so the windows are covered. Otherwise, your parakeet might panic and fly into the glass and hurt itself.

88 If your house has a fireplace, cover the opening with a screen or netting. If you have a dog or a cat, keep these pets away from your parakeet.

89 During the summer, turn off any fans that could hurt your pet. Also, remove house plants that could poison your pet.

90 To stay healthy, a parakeet should fly freely for a half hour each day. Leave the cage door open so your bird can return home. If your parakeet does not fly into its cage on its own, get it to hop onto your finger.

91 You can also put some fresh food, such as a piece of fruit, in the cage to tempt your bird inside. If your pet still does not go in, turn off the lights so you can catch it more easily.

92 To pick up your bird, carefully put your hand over its back and then cup it gently with both hands. Hold on to the bird firmly, so it feels safe, but do not squeeze your pet.

93 When checking your parakeet to see if it is healthy, hold the bird in one hand, with its head between your index and middle fingers. Use your other hand to gently examine your parakeet.

95 Your pet may take a long time — a few weeks or even longer — to learn to repeat its first word, so you will need to be patient.

94 You can teach your parakeet to repeat words, but you will need time and patience to bring out its talents. Start with a single word, such as the parakeet's name, and repeat it again and again.

97 The key to teaching your bird to talk is to repeat words and short sentences again and again. Keep your lessons to no more than 15 minutes at a time, and try to train your pet at a regular time each day.

96 If your parakeet repeats a word after you have said it, be sure to give your pet a tasty reward, like a small piece of carrot or apple.

28

98 Some parakeets learn words easily, while others take more time or never start to talk. Like people, each bird is different and has its own personality and way of learning.

99 You can also train your parakeet to do simple tricks, such as climbing a ladder or ringing a bell on a toy.

100 Teach your pet to do these tricks by using your finger to show it what you want it to do. In time, it will copy your actions.

101 Spend time talking to your parakeet, teach it tricks, and watch it at play. Lively, friendly, and intelligent, the parakeet is one of the most interesting pets to keep.

Glossary

albino: a white parakeet that lacks color in its feathers.

aviary: an outside enclosure for birds that is large enough for the birds to fly freely.

barring: fine, wavy black lines on a parakeet's head.

breeders: persons who raise a particular type or breed of animal.

cere: the featherless, fleshy area above a bird's beak.

crested: a type of parakeet that has a fringe of feathers sticking out around its head.

flight: an indoor enclosure large enough for birds to fly in.

gizzard: the part in a bird's body that grinds up tough food.

husk: the outer part of a seed, which parakeets do not eat.

kernel: the inner part of a seed.

lutino: an all-yellow bird with red eyes.

molt: to shed or lose old feathers.

pied: a parakeet with patches of color on its wings.

preen: to clean and straighten feathers with one's beak.

spangled: a parakeet with a solid body color and pale wings, which have dark edges.

tufted: a type of parakeet that has a crest at the front of its head.

warm-blooded: having a constant body temperature, usually warmer than the temperature of the surroundings.

More Books to Read

The Budgie: An Owner's Guide to a Happy Healthy Pet (Owner's Guide to a Happy Healthy Pet series) Julie Rach (Hungry Minds)

Birds (ASPCA Pet Care Guides for Kids series) Mark Evans (DK Publishing)

The Complete Book of Parakeet Care Annette Wolter (Barron's Educational Series)

Parakeets (Junior Pet Care series) Zuza Vrbova (Chelsea House)

Web Sites

The Budgie Place
www.geocities.com/budgie-place/

Budgerigars.com
www.budgerigars.com

English Budgies
www.parrotparrot.com/budgies/

Pet budgies
www.birds.about.com/pets/birds/library/blbudgie.htm

To find additional web sites, use a reliable search engine, such as www.yahooligans.com, with one or more of the following keywords: **budgerigars, parakeets, pet birds.**

Index